DATE DUE

Los Vaqueros

Our First Cowboys

Vaquero of the brush country, Southwest Texas, 1937.
Courtesy Center for American History

Los Vaqueros
Our First Cowboys

By
Sammye Munson

Eakin Press ★ Austin, Texas

Published in the United States of America
By Eakin Press
An Imprint of Sunbelt Media, Inc.
P. O. Drawer 90159 ★ Austin, TX 78709-0159

2   3   4   5   6   7   8   9

ISBN 1-57168-142-6

I want to tell you about myself and my family. We have always lived on ranches in the southwestern United States. My family lived here when it was part of Mexico. I like to hear my grandpa tell stories of the old days. He was a *vaquero*. His dad and grandpa were *vaqueros* before him. I am proud of them.

Here is my story.

Francisco

My name is Francisco. I live on a ranch in South Texas. The wind blows dust in my eyes as I watch my father work. He is an expert horseman and can rope calves as quick as lightning. I want to be a *vaquero* (pronounced vah *ker* oh), a cowboy, like him.

Vaqueros were the first men in America to herd cattle from the back of a horse. They were our first cowboys.

Reproduced from the Collections of the Library of Congress

Oops! This stubborn calf is trying to get away from me. I want to lead him to the corral where he belongs. My father smiles in approval, making sure I'm doing my job right. I learn from him as he learned from his father, my grandfather. Most of the men in my family have been vaqueros.

4

It's not easy to throw a loop around the calf's neck. It takes practice, just like playing baseball does. Practice is the only way I learn. I twirl my lariat above my head and toss it over the head of a calf.

6

My friends and I like growing up on a ranch. I am old enough to help my father. I help clean the corral where the horses exercise. My father is teaching me to rope and tie a calf.

Courtesy of the Dallas Museum of Art, gift of *Life* Magazine

My grandfather told me that the Spanish brought cattle and horses to New Spain (Mexico) over 450 years ago. Cortés, an explorer from Spain, chose a green valley in Mexico to begin raising cattle. The good grasslands produced healthy cattle that soon multiplied in number.

Courtesy of the Institute of Texan Cultures, San Antonio

The natives in Mexico worked for the Spanish leaders and learned their way of ranching. They were called *vaqueros*, after the word *vaca*, which means "cow" in Spanish. The men might have been Spanish, Mexican Indians, Mestizo (Spanish and Indian), or African. They used a pole to guide the cattle in early days.

Courtesy of *Texas Highways*

Long ago Catholic priests came from Spain to Mexico to teach religion to the natives. They built missions in areas that are now California and Texas. The natives who chose to live at the missions learned to read, weave cloth, and make pottery. They also learned to farm and to ranch. Money made from ranching supported the missions.

Courtesy of the Institute of Texan Cultures, San Antonio

Later, in 1821, Mexico won its independence from Spain. Most of the priests left, and the missions closed. Ranching came to an end at the missions. My ancestors continued to raise cattle, especially in the dry brushlands of South Texas.

Texas became independent from Mexico in 1836. Then, in 1845, it became a state. A war between Texas and Mexico in 1848 changed the borders. Land that had been in Mexico became part of the United States.

Courtesy of the Connor Museum, Kingsville

Americans from other states heard of the good grazing land in the West and Southwest. They left their homes and moved west, hoping to become ranchers.

Many Mexican people, like my great-great-grandfather, could no longer keep their land. They were sometimes forced to sell their land because they could not pay the taxes. They then worked for the new American landowners.

The newcomers learned much from the vaqueros. They liked the old Spanish war saddles so much that they made their own saddles the same way.

Reproduced from the Collections of the Library of Congress

18

The *vaqueros* followed the cattle over miles of land. They lived outdoors. Their roof was the sky, sometimes blue, sometimes an angry gray. Often rain-drops fell on the *vaqueros* and soaked their bedrolls. On warm nights they slept on the open ground with rolled-up blankets for pillows.

They called their outdoor home "el campo" (el comp o). It was like camping. The men took turns cooking over an open fire, stirring beans or venison stew.

Courtesy of the Institute of Texan Cultures, San Antonio

On special occasions the *vaqueros* would have contests to see who could ride a wild horse, called a *bronco*, the longest. Or they would see who was the fastest roper. These contests were called *"rodeos"* (ro day ohs). I like to watch rodeos today.

A long time ago, *vaqueros* rode *broncos* until they stopped bucking. This could take many minutes, longer than cowboys ride today. They did not receive a prize for their skills, just the pride in knowing they had done their best. After the contests the men often had a *fiesta* (fee es tah), or party.

Courtesy of the Connor Museum, Kingsville

My great-great-grandfather continued teaching American ranchers the old ways he knew so well. He worked long hours and could be gone for weeks, rounding up cattle or on trail drives. When he worked nearby, he lived with his wife and children in a one-room house near the main ranch. Called a "jacal" (hah kal), it had a thatched roof and dirt floor. Four poles set in a square held up walls made of wood.

Courtesy of the Connor Museum, Kingsville

My great-great-grandmother kept
the family together. She taught the children religion. She cooked and sewed.
She doctored those who became sick
and treated them with herbs she grew
in her garden.

Courtesy of the Center for American History

In early days there were no trains or trucks to take cattle to other states. Many people wanted the cows for food or to start their own ranches. The animals had to be taken on foot for hundreds of miles.

I try to imagine thousands of cows thundering through towns and over countrysides. The sounds of their hooves hitting the ground and the smell of their bodies let everyone know they were coming. They even crossed rivers to get to other states.

The Institute of Texan Cultures, San Antonio
Courtesy John Weldenthal Family

Black cowboys were also quick to learn how to ride, rope, and handle cattle. Before there were trains to transport the animals, cowboys or *vaqueros* guided them on foot for many miles to market. Black cowboys often became trail bosses, leading the others to faraway states such as Louisiana, Colorado, Kansas, and Oklahoma. They camped out on the open land on the trip.

A chuckwagon followed the trail bosses over dusty roads. It carried food and water for the *vaqueros*. The cook prepared hearty dishes like beans, tortillas, and venison stew. *Vaqueros* worked hard and needed good food to eat.

Courtesy of *Texas Highways*

Saddles from North Africa influenced the design of war saddles brought to America by the Spaniards. The high back kept the rider from sliding off the mount. This Moroccan saddle has changed over the years so that vaqueros can work with cattle more easily.

Saddles have always been important to vaqueros and cowboys. In early days they made their own from the limb of a tree. They carved it to suit them, then covered it with leather from animals.

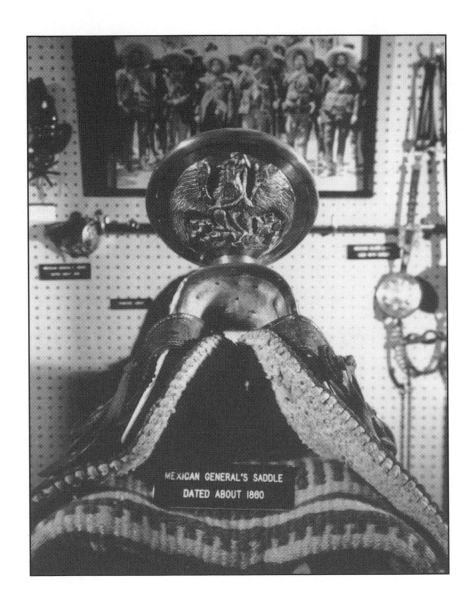

Courtesy of *Texas Highways*

I look at my dad's saddle and realize how much saddles have improved since the old days.

A Mexican general owned this saddle in the 1800s. It had a horn cap on top. Later, the Spanish *vaquero* replaced the horn cap with a saddle horn. He could tie his rope around the horn after he lassoed an animal. The saddle horn is still on saddles today.

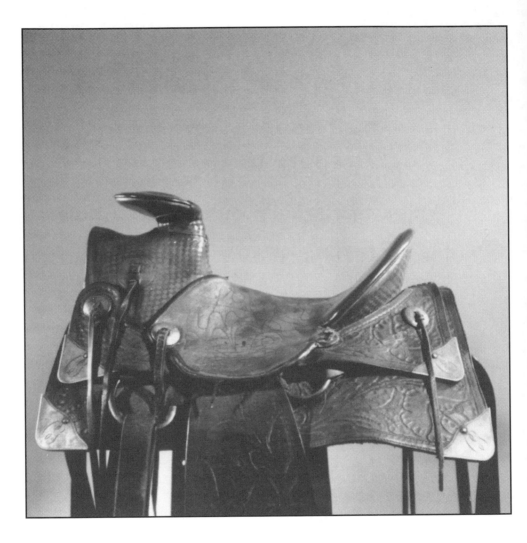

Courtesy of *Texas Highways*

I hope to have a fancy saddle of my own someday. A *vaquero* values his saddle. It is a prized possession and must be comfortable and fit his body. The modern saddle and its stirrups make it easier to herd cattle and rope calves.

Reproduced from the Collections of the Library of Congress

Cowboys still dress and act today much like the older ones did on trail drives. A cowboy is seldom without a hat. Sometimes called a *sombrero* (sum bray ro), it shields his face from the sun. It protects his head from the summer heat and winter winds.

A *sombrero* or cowboy hat can be used as a cup for drinking. Or as an umbrella when it rains. A cowboy can even fan himself with his hat.

Courtesy of *Texas Highways*

Can you imagine riding through cactus and mesquite trees without protecting your legs? *Vaqueros* and cowboys wore *"chaparreras"* (chop ah rare ahs), leather coverings over their pant legs. Some cowboys today wear short chaps, as this cowboy does.

Courtesy of *Texas Highways*

I wear boots now. Some cowboys wear lower heeled boots called "ropers." In early days my grandfather wore moccasins with spurs on the heels. Spurs are placed on boots to help nudge the horse or control his speed.

Courtesy of the Connor Museum, Kingsville

A *vaquero's* best friend was the lariat, or *la reata* (la ray ah tah). In early days these *reatas* were made of tough rawhide. *Vaqueros* braided six or eight strips of leather to make a strong lariat.

Today most lariats are made of stiff nylon. Yet in South Texas, some *vaqueros* like these in the photo still weave horsehair to make lariats. They like the old ways best.

Reproduced from the Collections of the Library of Congress

An important job Grandpa and other *vaqueros* had was rounding up cattle. During a roundup, *vaqueros* rode all over the big ranch. They looked for cattle and led them to one central place. Long ago there were no fences. Cattle roamed over many acres looking for good grass to eat.

Each *vaquero* had extra saddle horses to help with the cattle. Five to ten horses for each *vaquero* moved with him. This group of horses was called a *remuda* (ray *moo* dah).

Courtesy of *Texas Highways*

Sometimes calves need vaccinating so they do not get diseases. Cows often need doctoring. My grandfather would rope a calf and hold it while another *vaquero* inspected it.

Courtesy of *Texas Highways*

Vaqueros branded each new calf. Two men held the calf as another took a long-handled tool with the owner's initials on it. The vaquero heated the tool and placed it briefly on the back side of the calf. Seconds later, the calf scrambled off to its mother. If a calf was ever lost it was returned to the owner because of the initials.

As you can see in this photo, calves are still branded today.

Courtesy of *Texas Highways*

Sometimes *vaqueros* had dogs to help them round up cattle. These dogs had to be smart and well-trained. They ran beside the cows, keeping them together. The dogs never attacked the cattle. A good cattle dog is still valuable to the *vaquero* today.

Courtesy of *Texas Highways*

From saddles to chaps, today's cowboys have imitated the *vaqueros* from Mexico. Our modern ranchers use many of the same methods that the early *vaqueros* used. Without using the *vaquero*'s skills, ranchers in the United States could have failed.

Vaqueros today have different equipment. Fewer men are needed to work on ranches because of machinery and trucks. In South Texas the *vaquero* has new duties.

When I am a *vaquero*, I will need a hammer and pliers to work on machinery and the windmill. The windmill that pumps water from the ground is very important for cattle.

Courtesy of the Connor Museum, Kingsville

Instead of riding miles across the range all day on horseback, I may drive a pickup truck with a horse trailer behind. I will take the horse to a far part of the ranch and work the cattle. Of course, I will use my *reata* and sit on a saddle. At the end of the day, I will return to the main ranch instead of sleeping under the stars.

Courtesy of the Zintgraff Collection,
The Institute of Texan Cultures, San Antonio

Sometimes I look up and see helicopters above me. In some areas ranchers use them to help round up cattle. Cattle drives no longer exist. Trucks now transport cattle to other places.

Reproduced from the Collections of the Library of Congress

With all these improvements, though, I will still ride horseback and work cattle as my ancestors did hundreds of years ago.

I'll take my lasso, swing it round and round my head, and just at the right moment, sling it toward a calf. I'll watch the rope land perfectly around its neck. That is, if I keep on practicing.

Words of the Vaquero

el campo: outdoor camp

el mestizo: a person who is part Spanish and part Indian

el rodéo: contest of riding, roping skills

el sombrero: wide-brimmed hat

el jacal: one-room house

la fiesta: a party

la reata: lariat or lasso

la vaca: cow

los chaparreras: chaps, leather coverings over pant legs

Author's Note

The true story of *Los Vaqueros,* our first cowboys, dates back many years. They lived in Mexico, which then included much of the southwestern United States. Mexico lost the land that was Texas when Texas won independence in 1836. The Rio Grande became the border between the countries when Texas became a state in 1845.

Mexico refused to accept this boundary. A war began, and the United States sent troops into Mexico. The United States claimed land that is now California, New Mexico, and part of Arizona. The Rio Grande remained the boundary.

Americans flocked to Texas, and many of the settlers claimed land that had been given to the Spaniards and Mexicans as land grants.

The Mexican people in Texas had to accept a new language and new laws. A lack of understanding often led to unpaid taxes. Many Mexicans lost their land and began working for the new landowners. The Mexicans taught the newcomers the proper way to ranch. They were *Los Vaqueros,* our first cowboys.

Bibliography

Cisneros, José. *Riders of the Borderlands.* El Paso: The University of Texas at El Paso, 1981.

Dary, David. *Cowboy Culture.* Lawrence, KS: University of Kansas Press, 1989.

Erickson, John. "Saddle Up." *Texas Highways* 40, no. 6 (1984): 38-47.

Forbis, William H. *The Cowboys.* Alexandria, VA: Time-Life Books, 1978.

Graham, Joe. *El Rancho in South Texas, Continuity and Change from 1750.* Denton, TX: John E. Connor Museum, University of North Texas Press, 1994.

Jackson, Jack. *Los Mesteños: Spanish Ranching in Texas 1721-1821.* College Station: Texas A&M University Press, 1986.

Martin, Russell. *Enduring Myths of the Wild West.* New York: Stuart, Tabori and Chang, 1983.

McDowell, Bart. *The American Cowboy in Life and Legend.* Washington, DC: National Geographic Society, 1972.

Morrison, Dan. "The Right Gear." *Texas Highways* 40, no. 9 (1994): 7-15.

Wittliff, William D. *Genesis of the Texas Cowboy.* San Antonio: University of Texas Press, 1972.

Interviews:

Dr. Joe Graham, professor of anthropology and folklore, Texas A&I University, Kingsville, Texas.

Michael Moore, executive director, Ft. Bend Museum Association, George Ranch Historical Park, Richmond, Texas.